FOUND GUILTY

PAIRED:

Two women who refused to let injustice stand.
Myrlie Evers-Williams (left) kept track of
her husband's assassin for 30 years. Betty
Anne Waters put herself through law
school to free her brother from prison.

"After some years, people said: 'Myrlie, you're living in the past. Let it go.' But the fact that no one had been found guilty [of my husband's murder] made it hard to let go. I saw it as a moral issue. A society should not allow murderers to go free."

Myrlie Evers-Williams

"Not all people in prison are guilty like all of us are meant to believe. There's an element of human error with eyewitnesses and prosecutors. Too many people have too much power to do the wrong thing. We need more checks and balances for everybody in the system. Thank God for DNA."

Betty Anne Waters

Photographs © 2012: AP Images: 97 (Victoria Arocho), 58 (Jim Bourdier), back cover left, 3 left (Jennifer Graylock), 12, 29 (Francis H. Mitchell/Ebony Collection), 80 (Steven Senne), 57 bottom, 57 top (Rogelio V. Solis), 24 (Neal Ulevich), back cover right, 3 right (Chris Young, The Canadian Press), 10, 38; Corbis Images: 19, 34, 46 (Bettmann), 44 (Flip Schulke); Getty Images: 50 (William F. Campbell/Time Life Pictures), 90 (Stephen Ferry); Library of Congress, Prints and Photographs Division: 16; Media Bakery: cover background; NEWSCOM/Christine Chew/ UPI: 100; ShutterStock, Inc.: cover inset (Nata-Lia), 60 (Lou Oates); The Granger Collection, New York: 32; The Innocence Project: 67, 70, 72, 75, 84, 88, 93; Wikipedia/John Phelan: 62.

Library of Congress Cataloging-in-Publication Data

Midland, C. J.
Found guilty / C.J. Midland.
p. cm. -- (On the record)
Includes bibliographical references and index.
ISBN-13: 978-0-531-22555-4 (pbk.)
ISBN-10: 0-531-22555-0
1. Trials (Murder)--United States--Juvenile literature. 2. Judicial error--United States--Juvenile literature. 3. Evers, Medgar Wiley, 1925-1963--Assassination--Juvenile literature. 4. Evers-Williams, Myrlie--Juvenile literature. 5. Waters, Betty Ann--Juvenile literature. 6. Waters, Kenny--Trials, litigation, etc.--Juvenile literature. 7. Waters, Kenny I. Title.
KF221.M8M53 2012
345.73'02523--dc22

2011016942

Tod Olson, Series Editor
Marie O'Neill, Creative Director
Curriculum Concepts International, Production
Thanks to Candy J. Cooper

FOUND GUILTY

They held out for justice when
everyone else had given up.

C. J. Midland

Contents

LONG ROAD TO JUSTICE

In 1963 Myrlie Evers watched her husband die from an assassin's bullet. She knew Mississippi wasn't ready to convict a white man for the murder of a black man. But that didn't mean she had to accept the verdict.

The Evers family visits a Civil War battlefield in Vicksburg, Mississippi, in 1958. Myrlie Evers-Williams (then Myrlie Evers) stands with her husband, Medgar Evers, and their children Reena and Darrell.

1

Warning Shot

The faint sound of a car rumbled outside the tiny ranch house in Jackson, Mississippi. It was close to midnight on May 28, 1963. Myrlie Evers tilted an ear toward her bedroom window.

Fear had sharpened her senses in recent months. Evers's husband, Medgar, had become the leading voice for civil rights in a state where many white people hated African Americans. It was only a matter of time, Myrlie felt, before that hatred was turned on the Evers family.

Medgar knew it too. He had warned Myrlie one night as she sat on their couch, her back to the picture window. "Keep sitting there," he said, "and you're going to have your head blown off."

Medgar was working late, as he often did. The children were asleep in their rooms. The house was quiet. Outside, the car seemed to have stopped.

A second later the sound of shattering glass broke the silence. Then Evers heard an explosion. She ran from her bedroom to see flames leaping from the garage.

Evers ran outside in her slip and grabbed the garden hose. She put out the fire before it reached the gas tank of her car.

When the police arrived, they looked around the charred garage. The damage had been done by a firebomb. It was home-made, but it could have burned the whole house down.

Like all the police in Mississippi, the officers at the scene were white. At first they suggested that Evers might have started the fire herself. Then they refused to admit that the incident was more than a harmless prank.

By this time, Medgar had heard about the fire and rushed home. When the police and the neighbors finally left, he took Myrlie in his arms. He could not live with himself if his work brought harm to his family, he told her.

"It's not us," Myrlie said, finally letting the tears flow. "It's you they're after. And if anything happened to you, I don't think I could live."

A man walks up to the blacks-only balcony in a segregated movie theater in Mississippi in 1962. Slavery ended in 1865, but in the late 1870s southern states began to pass so-called Jim Crow laws to deny blacks the same rights as whites.

2

A Good Girl

Rebellion did not come naturally to Myrlie Beasley Evers. She grew up in Vicksburg, Mississippi, in a strict, middle-class family. As she explained in her memoir *Watch Me Fly*, obedience was expected, and she learned her duties well.

Her mother was just 16 when she gave birth to Myrlie in 1933. Myrlie's paternal grandmother, Annie Beasley, took charge of the baby. Myrlie called her Mama. Later, her aunt Myrlie Polk stepped in to help raise her. Both Mama and Aunt Myrlie were schoolteachers. They gave their precious girl music lessons, taught her perfect diction, and introduced her to classic works of literature.

They showered Myrlie with love—and whipped her with a switch when she misbehaved. She had to sit stone-still in church. She had to walk, not run, in the house. She had to make sure there wasn't a speck of dust on the shelves.

When Myrlie was growing up, racism was as stifling as the humid southern air. Segregation—the separation of blacks and whites—was the law of the land. Jim Crow laws, as they were called, kept the races apart in all public facilities. Whites had privileges that blacks were forced to

Images of separate drinking fountains for blacks and whites became symbolic of segregation in the South.

go without—nice parks, libraries, public swimming pools. In Mississippi, black children couldn't attend the same schools as white children. And most black students had to make do with tattered textbooks and crumbling classrooms.

Black citizens had almost no power to change the laws. There were no black police officers, judges, or jury members. It was nearly impossible for a black person to vote in the South. They were driven from the polls, either by outright violence or by laws demanding that they pay a tax or take an impossibly difficult test. From 1901 to 1973, no southern state sent a black legislator to the U.S. Congress.

Yet in Myrlie's home, no one complained about the injustices. Her family seemed to accept the world the way it was. Myrlie rode the bus when she had to—jammed into the rows behind the "Coloreds Only" sign. At the movie theater, she sat with her black friends in the balcony.

Myrlie knew hardly any white people besides the Robinsons, the family that employed her maternal grandmother, Alice Washington. Washington cleaned the brick mansion that belonged to the Robinsons. Myrlie visited the house every year around Christmas to play the piano. After Myrlie played, Mrs. Robinson gave her a gift and a bag of gumdrops. The experience made Myrlie feel like an important guest—except for one thing, which she hated. She had to come and go through the back door.

At her high school, Myrlie graduated second in her class. She wanted to become a concert pianist, but there was no black public college in the state with a music program. She enrolled at Alcorn Agricultural and Mechanical College, an all-black school in rural Lorman, Mississippi.

By now, 17-year-old Myrlie Beasley had grown tall and attractive. On the drive to Alcorn in the fall of 1950, Mama filled her with warnings.

"Baby, now you be a good girl," Mama ordered as they hugged each other good-bye, "and don't get involved with any of those veterans."

Some 85,000 black men from Mississippi had fought in World War II. Many of them had enrolled in college when they returned. These men were older and more worldly than most college students. Mama was convinced they would corrupt innocent girls like Myrlie.

"Yes, Mama," Myrlie responded.

An hour or so later, she stood in a group of freshmen outside the college president's house. She was leaning against a lamppost in her first pair of high-heeled shoes. She watched the football team trot by. Her eyes fell on a tall, strikingly handsome athlete.

He saw her, too. "I think you better get off that light post," said Medgar Evers, a veteran with a devilish smile. "You might get electrocuted."

Myrlie tossed her long hair over her shoulder and raised an eyebrow.

"Oh," she said, trying to look mature, "I'm not worried."

Mound Bayou, Mississippi, was founded by a group of
former slaves in 1887. Medgar Evers was living there
when he got involved with the Civil Rights Movement.
He led boycotts against gas stations where blacks
were not allowed to use the restrooms.

Myrlie Beasley and Medgar Evers married in 1951. They lived at Alcorn College until Medgar graduated. When an insurance company hired Medgar, they moved to Mound Bayou, a tiny all-black town in the Mississippi Delta.

In his new job, Medgar drove around the Delta selling health, life, and burial insurance to black sharecroppers. His clients were farmers who rented land from white owners and paid for it with some of the crops they raised. They lived in conditions unlike anything Medgar had seen. On his sales calls he met families of 12 crowded into small, leaky shacks. He'd come home and share his outrage with Myrlie. He had to *do* something, he told her.

Myrlie found it hard to be encouraging. She was caught up in her own unhappiness. She had left college without a degree, disappointing Mama and Aunt Myrlie. She was bored to death with her typing job and with Mound Bayou. It was a backwater town that seemed to offer her nothing.

In 1955 Myrlie and Medgar Evers moved to Jackson, Mississippi, where Medgar had a new job. He had agreed to open a Mississippi office for the National Association for the Advancement of Colored People (NAACP). The organization was the most powerful civil rights group in the country, waging a battle for the rights of African Americans.

The NAACP chipped away at racial inequality by winning court battles and striking down laws that enforced Jim Crow. Just a year earlier, NAACP lawyers had won a major case known as *Brown v. Board of Education of Topeka*. In *Brown*, the Supreme Court ruled that the segregation of public schools was illegal. The southern states would have to allow black and white students to go to school together.

News of the decision rumbled through the South like an earthquake. It had the potential to tear apart the entire system of racial segregation. But getting rid of Jim Crow would take a lot of work—and Medgar Evers wanted to do his part.

In Jackson, Medgar and Myrlie Evers got the new NAACP office up and running. Medgar went to work investigating cases of violence against black people. Myrlie did secretarial work in the office.

Myrlie was happy to leave Mound Bayou behind for a bigger, livelier city. She also found her work at the NAACP far more interesting than her typing job. And it opened her eyes to the injustices of life in Mississippi.

Still, she felt like she was living in Medgar's shadow. They had two small children to raise now, Darrell and Reena. Medgar was rarely home to help. He traveled the state gathering testimony about chilling acts of violence. It was already obvious that he was taking big risks.

This 1958 photograph shows Medgar Evers with his daughter, Reena, at their home in Jackson, Mississippi.

Since the *Brown* ruling, Mississippi had become a battleground in a new struggle for civil rights. The ruling gave activists the opportunity to attack segregation laws. In response, racist politicians and businessmen formed groups known as Citizens' Councils to defend Jim Crow. They made sure that black activists who tried to vote or joined protests lost their jobs. They boycotted businesses that hired black workers and newspapers that criticized segregation.

Medgar had trouble keeping up with the relentless wave of threats and murders. In May 1955 he investigated the death of Reverend George Lee, a grocery store owner who was active in the NAACP. Lee was shot by a carload of white men while driving home one Saturday night.

Then came the August 13 murder of Lamar Smith. He was shot dead after organizing blacks to vote by absentee ballot.

Two weeks later, a 14-year-old boy from Chicago named Emmett Till was murdered. He had come to Mississippi for the summer to visit his uncle. His mangled body was found floating in the Tallahatchie River. His offense? Supposedly he had flirted with a white woman in a store.

The murders helped ignite a storm of anger across the South. Over the next few years, that anger grew into a powerful protest movement. It started with a bus boycott in Montgomery, Alabama. The boycott led to sit-ins, marches, and massive rallies. The protesters made the quiet acceptance of Mama and Aunt Myrlie seem old-fashioned. A new

Sit-ins were a common way to protest segregation during the 1950s and 1960s. Activists would sit in segregated areas and refuse to move. Here, four young men sit at a segregated lunch counter in Jackson. They are about to be arrested by the police.

generation was determined to make a stand against segregation.

Medgar Evers made his stand in Jackson. He registered voters and urged them to go to the polls. He organized parents to demand integrated schools for their children. In 1962 he pushed the University of Mississippi to accept James Meredith, its first black student.

During the spring of 1963, Medgar helped organize a boycott of Jackson's white-owned businesses. Protesters demanded that business owners hire black workers and serve black customers. In May a group of black and white students held a sit-in at a segregated lunch counter in downtown Jackson. They were beaten by a white mob while police stood by and watched.

The following night, the firebomb exploded in the Everses' garage.

Medgar Evers (with sign) and NAACP executive secretary
Roy Wilkins are arrested for protesting outside a Woolworth's
store on June 1, 1963. The protest was part of Evers's boycott
of the segregated businesses in downtown Jackson.

In the weeks to come, Myrlie was beside herself with fear. When Medgar left in the morning, she had no idea whether she would see him again. She slept with a gun on her nightstand and fielded hate calls. "That n----- husband of yours is going to get himself killed if he doesn't watch his step," one anonymous caller sneered.

"Hate like that will build up inside you until it poisons you," Myrlie responded. More often, she just hung up.

To Myrlie's horror, Medgar began training the children in self-defense. Darrell was nine now, and Reena was eight. Their second son, Van, was just three. Medgar taught the kids to listen for cars and fall to the floor, infantry style. They could no longer sit on the furniture to watch television. They watched from the floor.

"Where is the safest place to go if you hear gunshots?" Medgar asked Darrell and Reena.

"The bathtub, Daddy!" Darrell said proudly. "The bathtub!" Reena parroted.

The threatening phone calls grew more frequent. The house would be blown up, one caller said. Medgar had hours to live, said another. One man said he had a pistol. Medgar could hear the cylinder of a revolver spin in the background. "This is for you," the man told Medgar.

But Medgar kept working. In the weeks after the firebombing, he put in 20-hour days. On June 11 he kissed Myrlie and the children and walked out to his car. A few minutes later he returned and kissed them again. "Myrlie, I'm so tired," he said. "I don't think I can make it, but I can't stop either."

That evening Myrlie let the children stay up late to wait for their father. President John F. Kennedy was giving a speech about civil rights, and she watched with the children. Van fell asleep, and Myrlie nodded off. Darrell was the first to hear his father.

"Here comes Daddy," he exclaimed.

What would Medgar say about Kennedy's speech? Myrlie wondered. The soothing sound of Medgar's Oldsmobile drew near. She knew the progression by heart, like a favorite song. The tires crunched across the driveway gravel. The car engine shut off. The driver's door creaked open. It slammed shut, and then . . .

A gunshot rang out, thunderous and ugly. After that, there was silence.

Jackson Police Captain Ralph Hargrove studies the rifle used to kill Medgar Evers. The weapon was found near the Evers home.

4
Justice Denied

At the sound of the gunshot, the children hit the floor and crawled toward the bathtub. Myrlie ran to the door. Medgar lay facedown, covered in blood. His hand, clutching the house keys, stretched toward the door. T-shirts lay scattered around him, printed with the antisegregation slogan "Jim Crow Must Go." He had been shot once in the back. Myrlie's piercing scream brought the children running.

"Daddy, get up," they begged, hovering over their father. "Please get up."

Myrlie rushed to the phone and called the police. Neighbors arrived. Soon sirens shrieked and police lights scanned the lawn. Someone grabbed Reena's mattress, put Medgar on it, and lifted him into a station wagon. The car took off for the hospital. Another neighbor gathered the crying children while Myrlie went inside and prayed.

A short time later, Myrlie's friend Hattie Tate walked in with a drawn face. "Is he gone?" Myrlie asked. Hattie couldn't speak. Myrlie slumped to the floor.

Distraught as she was, Evers insisted on speaking the following night to a large gathering of civil rights supporters. At a local church, she stood in the glare of television lights before a crowd of hundreds.

"I come to you tonight with a broken heart," she began. She talked about how much Medgar had worked and sacrificed. Let others draw strength, courage, and determination from his life, she said. He would want them to finish the fight.

As for finding her husband's assassin, Evers had little faith in that fight. *It would be a miracle if there were ever an arrest*, she thought. Still, she found herself vowing, *I'm going to make whoever did this pay.*

The next morning detectives found a hunting rifle in a nest of vines across from the Evers house. The gun's barrel was the right size to have fired the bullet that killed Medgar Evers. Police lifted a fresh thumbprint from the scope of the rifle. The rifle, scope, and print were traced to one man—Byron de la

Beckwith. He was a 43-year-old fertilizer salesman and a gun collector.

Beckwith hated African Americans. He once wrote a letter to the National Rifle Association saying, "We here in Mississippi are going to have to do a lot of shooting to protect our wives, children, and ourselves from bad n------."

To Myrlie Evers's great surprise, the FBI arrested Beckwith and put him on trial. In January and February of 1964, a jury of 12 white men listened to the evidence, including Evers's description of the shooting. As Evers spoke, Mississippi's governor, Ross Barnett, walked over to Beckwith and gave him an encouraging pat on the back. Beckwith smirked through most of the trial. He seemed confident that the jury would find him innocent.

On a Thursday the jurors retreated behind closed doors to decide Beckwith's fate. Under the law, every member of the jury would have to agree on a verdict. By Friday morning they had argued for 11 hours and could not reach a unanimous decision. The judge declared a mistrial. They would have to start over.

Evers was shocked to learn that five white Mississippians had voted to convict Beckwith. "The fact that they could not agree signifies something," she told a reporter.

A second trial began in April. Again 12 white men deliberated, and again they couldn't agree. The judge declared a second mistrial, and Beckwith was released, though no one had actually declared him innocent.

When he returned to his hometown of Greenwood that evening, crowds lined the streets and cheered, as if greeting a hero.

Myrlie Evers attends her husband's funeral. Four thousand people were at the service, including well-known activists like Martin Luther King Jr.

5

"It's Not Over"

After the trials, Myrlie Evers tried to go on with her life. The NAACP invited her to speak to groups around the country. As it turned out, she had a talent for public speaking. She drew crowds and made tens of thousands of dollars for the association. People told her she was holding up well, but in truth she felt unbearably depressed.

Without Medgar, Myrlie struggled to find a reason to live. On her way home from her speaking trips, she drove recklessly.

GATION MUST GO

Myrlie Evers speaks at an NAACP rally at Howard University in Washington, D.C., just three months after her husband's murder.

She stockpiled sleeping pills. One night she almost tipped the whole bottle into her mouth.

In these dark months, the children kept her going. Her youngest child, Van, slept on the bed next to her. One night she lay there watching him sleep, so small and vulnerable. How could she think of leaving him alone in the world? "I can't do this," she said aloud.

From that day forward, Evers vowed to get her life back on track. She had promised Medgar that she would care for their children. In her speeches she had urged audiences to keep Medgar's name alive. It was time for her to live up to her own words.

To make a fresh start, Evers moved the family to Southern California, settling in the college town of Claremont. Her children attended excellent schools. Evers enrolled at Pomona College, one of the best small colleges in the country. She earned a bachelor's degree in sociology and went to work for the Claremont Colleges. She ran for public office, something her husband had never done. And she eventually took a high-powered job in public relations at an oil company.

Evers had cast off her good-girl, get-along image. She succeeded in business and public life and raised her three children alone. She also met a new man, Walter Williams. They fell in love and married in 1976.

In the back of her mind, though, Myrlie Evers-Williams had unfinished business. She returned often to Mississippi and kept track of Byron de la Beckwith. She looked for a way to reopen the case.

Beckwith was rumored to have talked about the murder to friends. *Keep talking,* Evers-Williams thought. *One of these days you're going to give yourself away.*

On the twenty-fifth anniversary of her husband's assassination, Evers-Williams attended a ceremony at Arlington National Cemetery. Van, who was now 28, went with her. It was his first visit to his father's grave. Mother and son stood in front of the grave for a long time, and Van started to cry. She took him in her arms, as she had when he was a boy, and rocked him.

She said to herself, *No, it's not over.*

In 1994 Byron de la Beckwith was tried for the third time for the murder of Medgar Evers. Here state troopers escort the then 73-year-old Beckwith to court.

6

A Final Verdict

One day in 1989, Evers-Williams received a call from Jerry Mitchell, a newspaper reporter from Mississippi. Mitchell had uncovered new information about the murder case. Government employees may have tampered with the jury in Beckwith's second trial, he said. They had checked into the racial views of potential jurors and told Beckwith's lawyers what they discovered.

The reporter asked Evers-Williams whether the new information should lead to a third trial of Beckwith. "Yes!" she exclaimed.

Nearly three decades had passed since Medgar Evers's murder, and Mississippi had changed. There were no more "whites only" bathrooms in the courthouse or anywhere else. New laws had forced integration and transformed the justice system. Black Mississippians voted and sat on juries. They served as police officers and district attorneys. In Beckwith's first trial, the prosecutor had asked potential jurors whether they thought "killing a n-----" was a crime. In a new trial, that would never be asked.

Myrlie Evers-Williams began to pressure Mississippi officials to reopen the case. A few officials were more than willing. She got in touch with an assistant district attorney named Bobby DeLaughter. DeLaughter was already looking for new evidence and witnesses. They spoke every week to discuss his progress. Before long a third trial date was set.

In January 1994, 30 years after the first trial, Evers-Williams testified for a third time about the night of her late husband's death.

Beckwith looked all of his 73 years. He had large square glasses and thin, graying hair. He listened soberly as the trial proceeded. New witnesses testified that over the decades he had bragged about killing Medgar Evers. Prosecutors read his racist writings to the jury. Beckwith had compared African Americans to boll weevils, the insects that devour cotton crops. Black people, he had written, "must be destroyed and their remains burned."

Listening to the testimony, Evers-Williams felt physically ill. "You would think after years and years I would be immune to it," she told a reporter. "I'm not."

This time eight of the 12 jurors were African American. The jury began deliberations on a Friday afternoon. Evers-Williams and the prosecutors paced the halls as the hours ticked by. A rainstorm raged outside. The next morning the storm worsened, and by 10:20 A.M. on February 5, 1994, word spread that the jury had reached its verdict.

Evers-Williams filed into the courtroom with her son Darrell and her daughter,

Reena. The clerk read the verdict. "We find the defendant guilty." Cheers erupted around her and echoed through the halls of the courthouse. Crying with joy, the family embraced the prosecutors and each other. A short while later, Evers-Williams searched for a way to express the layers of feeling.

"All I want to do," she began quietly, smiling through her tears, "is say, 'Yea, Medgar!'" Her voice trembled and rose. She threw her arms in the air and pumped her fists: "Yea! Yea! Yea!" Then she grabbed her forehead with both hands and covered her eyes.

"Medgar's life was not in vain," she said, regaining her composure. "Perhaps he did more in death than he could have in life. Somehow I think he is still among us."

In 1995 Evers-Williams was chosen to lead the NAACP, 40 years after her husband had opened the office in Jackson. She founded an institute to keep Medgar's memory alive. And she returned to Jackson to dedicate a post office to her husband. Two blocks away, Byron de la Beckwith sat behind bars in the county detention center. He died in prison seven years later, at age 80.

Like the state of Mississippi, Myrlie Evers-Williams had come a long way since Medgar was murdered. The conviction of her husband's killer had taken her that much further.

"When it was over, every pore was wide open and the demons left," she said. "I was reborn when that jury said 'Guilty.'"

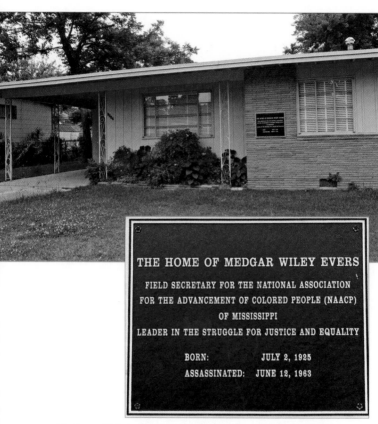

THE HOME OF MEDGAR WILEY EVERS

FIELD SECRETARY FOR THE NATIONAL ASSOCIATION
FOR THE ADVANCEMENT OF COLORED PEOPLE (NAACP)
OF MISSISSIPPI
LEADER IN THE STRUGGLE FOR JUSTICE AND EQUALITY

BORN: JULY 2, 1925
ASSASSINATED: JUNE 12, 1963

Myrlie and Medgar Evers and their three children lived
in this house in Jackson, Mississippi. This plaque on the
front of the house commemorates Medgar Evers's life.

Myrlie Evers speaks at a church in Jackson, Mississippi, 16 hours after Medgar Evers was assassinated. Years later, after her husband's killer was convicted, she read in a local paper that due in part to her efforts to bring justice to her family, "Mississippi is free at last."

Myrlie Evers-Williams

Born:

March 17, 1933

Grew up:

Vicksburg, Mississippi

Life's work:

Civil rights activist, community leader

Honors include:

The National Freedom Award
Ms. Magazine's Woman of the Year

Author of:

*Watch Me Fly: What I Learned on the Way to
Becoming the Woman I Was Meant to Be,*
with Melinda Blau
For Us, the Living, with William Peters

She says:

"For thirty years my focus had not wavered.
Like a tree deeply rooted on the banks of a
rushing river, *I had not moved.* While raising
my children, going to school, working my way
through the halls of power, even falling in love
again, I had stayed the battle."

THE PACT

Betty Anne Waters couldn't believe it
when her brother was convicted of murder.
But there he was, in jail for life. To save
him from despair, she gave him her word:
no matter how long it took,
she would get him out.

Kenny and Betty Anne Waters grew up here, in Ayer, Massachusetts. Kenny was living in Ayer when he was arrested for murder.

7
Booked

The telephone jolted Betty Anne Waters out of an early morning sleep. It was her older brother, Kenneth Waters, and he sounded agitated. He got right to the alarming point: he was in jail. Police officers in his hometown of Ayer, Massachusetts, had just arrested him for murder.

"What are they *doing*?" Betty Anne wondered aloud to her brother. Kenny had been her childhood idol and best friend. This had to be a mistake, and she assured him they would quickly set it straight.

Betty Anne hung up the phone and got dressed. It was October 12, 1982. She was 28 years old, a high school dropout and stay-at-home mom. Her husband owned a struggling real estate company. They were getting ready to sell their home in Rhode Island and start over in Florida.

That morning, however, Betty Anne had only one concern. She had to help her brother right away. She jumped in the car and began the drive to Ayer, 90 minutes northwest of Boston.

As she drove, she tried to figure out why Kenny had been arrested. The crime he was being charged with was two and a half years old. She remembered it well. A neighbor of Kenny's, Katharina Brow, had been found dead in her mobile home. Brow had been brutally beaten and stabbed. The linen closet, where she stashed her savings in an envelope, had been ransacked. Her cash and her jewelry were gone. The kitchen faucet had been left running. There was blood on the curtain behind the sink and throughout the trailer. There had obviously been a struggle.

With very few leads to guide the investigation, the police had treated Kenny as a possible suspect. He had lived next door to Brow with his girlfriend and their baby. He worked as a cook at the Park Street Diner. Brow had been a customer there and had talked about a large sum of money she was saving for a trip. Kenny also had a police record, with a conviction for slashing a man in New Hampshire with a knife.

The police investigated Kenny Waters but failed to link him to the murder. Kenny had no bloodstains on his clothes or cuts on his body. His alibi seemed airtight. He was working at the diner on the morning of the murder. After his shift he went home and put on a three-piece suit. Then he went to the courthouse in Ayer, where he was facing a charge of assaulting a police officer from a previous incident. (The assault charge was eventually dropped.)

Betty Anne was certain that Kenny was innocent. Besides the lack of evidence, she knew her brother well and believed he was incapable of murder. A year apart in age, they had stuck together while growing up in a chaotic family of nine children. The Waters family was poor, uneducated, and "dysfunctional," as Betty Anne says. The children had many different fathers, none

Seven of the Waters children pose for a photo at their mother's house in 1964. Betty Anne is at the top right, and Kenny is holding the dog.

of whom had stuck around for very long. At the time of Kenny's arrest, no one in the Waters family had been to college.

As kids, Kenny and Betty Anne were "rascals," she says. They skipped school, stole candy, and broke into neighbors' homes to play house. They were placed in foster care together and then painfully separated.

Around adults they often assumed roles—Kenny as the rabble-rouser, Betty Anne as his caretaker. Kenny was in second grade when his teacher brought him into Betty Anne's first-grade classroom. "Betty Anne, make him act like you!" the teacher said.

As an adult, Kenny Waters could be kind, considerate, and generous. But Betty Anne also knew his dark side. He had a hot temper, especially when he drank. He was the kind of troublemaker who cursed at cops and got into bar fights. But he was no murderer; Betty Anne was certain of that.

The police reopened the Brow case in October 1982, based on new evidence from two of Kenny's former girlfriends. Both women claimed that Kenny had told them he'd killed Katharina Brow. With their statements in hand, the Ayer police arrested Kenny Waters.

On the drive to Ayer, Betty Anne put her mind to work: she would find the time card from the diner to prove that Kenny could not have been at Brow's home at the time of the murder. She rolled up to an office building in Ayer where the diner's owner kept his records.

By PATRICIA W. MONTMINY
Sun Staff

AYER – The suspect in the murder of Katarina Brow had problems with alcohol and drugs, and spent three years in a New Hampshire jail for slashing the throat of a New Hampshire man, according to lawyers for the prosecution and defense.

Kenneth Waters, 29, of 28 Erie St., who police say was always a suspect in the Brow murder, was arraigned in Ayer District Court yesterday afternoon before Judge David Williams on charges of murder and armed robbery.

Waters, an unemployed short order cook, divorced, and the father of two children, was held without bail and remanded to the Billerica House of Correction after Asst. DA Neil Hasenstaf outlined Waters' personal history which included violence, drinking, and drugs.

Waters, whose case was continued to Oct. 20, was arrested Monday night at his mother's home in Providence by Ayer police officers Dennis MacDonald and Nancy Taylor.

He is charged in connection with the May 21, 1980, brutal slaying of Mrs. Brow, 48, inside her trailer at 7½ Rosewood Ave.

Hasenstaf told the court that Waters "has a long record of violence, and served time in a New Hampshire jail on charges that were reduced to aggravated assault."

According to officer Taylor, who has worked on the murder probe with Ayer Police Chief Philip Connors, the suspect was originally charged with attempted murder after slashing the throat of a New Hampshire man. As a result, he spent three years in jail after the incident happened in Rockingham County in 1978, she said.

Entering a plea of innocent in behalf of his client, defense counsel Stanley Narkounas admitted that Waters has had a history of "prob-

lems with alcohol and drugs, but he is willing to submit to a lie detector test."

But, Waters once failed to take a lie detector test.

As Hasenstaf told the court that Waters had "disappeared," and "was no where to be found" when police scheduled a polygraph, Waters announced "I'll take one right ..."

Narkounas asked for $20,000 bail on the grounds that Waters had returned to Ayer twice since the Brow slaying, once for a pending court matter.

Waters was fired from his job as a short order cook at the Park Street Diner in Ayer in September of 1980, Narkounas said.

He returned to Providence for several months, then went to California. After leaving California, Hasenstaf said, he went to Phoenix, Arizona where he remained for a year in a detoxification center.

MURDER SUSPECT KENNETH WATERS
...is led into the Ayer police station by officer Nancy Taylor yesterday afternoon.
Sun Staff Photo by Bob Whitak

Hasenstaf requested Waters be held without bail because he had been previously questioned by state and local police as a suspect in the Brow murder.

"This is a serious offense," Hasenstaf told Judge Williams, "the victim was killed in her own home. Thousands of dollars was stolen. A lie detector test was scheduled and he was no where to be found. He has a long record of violence and has served time in a New Hampshire jail."

Hasenstaf also told the court that Waters had defaulted a court appearance in Shrewsbury.

About five months ago Chief Connors reopened the Brow murder investigation after receiving what he called "some important information."

The probe escalated over the past two weeks, according to officer MacDonald, after "an informant came forward." MacDonald said

the informant would be testifying in court.

In addition to the information police have also acquired new physical evidence, Taylor said; however, police would not disclose what that evidence is.

Waters was born in Groton, and raised in Providence. Police said spent a considerable amount of time at the home of his late grandfather, Benjamin Davenport, who lived on Vernon Street, behind the Brow residence. Waters was living with his grandfather at the time of the murder, Taylor said.

Waters was arrested in the cell of his mother's home, Taylor said. He told police he was aware that was being sought, but that he was innocent and has an alibi, Taylor added.

Judge Williams declared Waters indigent and said he will assign a lawyer from the Massachusetts Public Defenders Committee next Wednesday.

The *Sun*, a Massachusetts newspaper, published an article about Kenny Waters's arrest. The reporter wrote about Waters's former criminal offenses and his problems with drugs and alcohol.

"Do you still have Kenny's time card?" Betty Anne asked the office worker who came to the counter.

"The police are on their way to pick it up right now," the woman answered.

Fine, Betty Anne thought. *Let the police have the time card.* They already knew that Kenny was in court later that morning. Could there be a more perfect alibi?

This mug shot of Kenny Waters was taken after he was arrested for the murder of Katharina Brow. He was 29 years old at the time.

8

The Promise

In May 1983, seven months after Kenny's arrest, Betty Anne Waters sat with her family in a small courtroom in Cambridge, Massachusetts. Kenny sat at the defense table with his lawyer. He wore the same dark blue suit he had worn the morning of Brow's murder. He had no money, so the court had appointed a lawyer to represent him.

Kenny had been told to stay calm, and he took his lawyer's advice. No eye-rolling, no outbursts. He just sat and stroked his dark beard. It must have been hard to listen to lies from witnesses without reacting, Betty Anne thought.

Brenda Marsh, one of Kenny's former girl-friends, gave the most damaging testimony: "I asked him if he killed that woman, and he said, 'Yeah, what's it to ya?'"

Betty Anne kept waiting for the time card to surface as evidence. But the document had never made it into the hands of Kenny's defense lawyer. Still, she expected the jury to see through the lies. Her mother was so certain that Kenny would be found innocent that she planned to buy the defense attorney a new briefcase.

After five days of testimony, the jury began deliberating. Betty Anne nervously walked the halls of the courthouse. She rode the elevator to the cafeteria. She drank

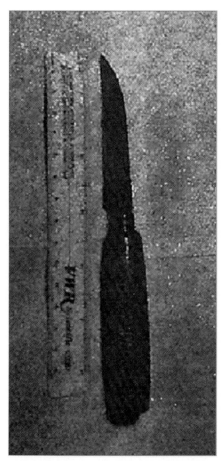

The murder weapon, a common, wood-handled knife, was used as evidence against Kenny Waters. Witnesses claimed a knife like it had gone missing from the warehouse where Kenny worked.

coffee and talked with her family. Two days passed before the jury returned with its verdict. The Waters family settled in the gallery benches, anxious to take Kenny home. The court clerk read the decision quickly: guilty of first-degree murder; guilty of armed robbery. The charges carried a sentence of life in prison.

Court officers handcuffed Kenny and led him away. The family had a moment in a small room to say good-bye before he was taken to prison. Betty Anne tried to sound optimistic.

"We're just going to have to get the appeal," she told him. But inside, she felt like she was dying.

Kenny went to prison. He told everyone there, from his doctors to other inmates, that he was innocent. He didn't have it in him to kill a person, he said.

"We were not raised like that," he later explained to a reporter. "You just do not hurt people like that." He'd get into fights in a bar, he admitted. "But I'd never kill anybody."

Kenny went downhill fast in prison. He suffered miserably. He grew so depressed that he began cutting his wrists and ankles. To protest his imprisonment, he refused to clean up his cell. The guards threw him into solitary confinement.

Betty Anne did her best to keep Kenny's spirits up. They talked by phone at least once a week, sometimes more. The family spent their last dollars trying to appeal the case. But one by one, the appeals were denied.

In 1986 yet another appeal failed. After the news came in, Betty Anne didn't hear from Kenny for a month. When he finally called he told her he had been so depressed that he had attempted suicide. Prison officials had put him in solitary for a month.

Betty Anne was angry and worried. She made Kenny promise that he would keep himself alive.

Kenny agreed, on one condition. "Betty Anne, I can't live here for the rest of my life for something I didn't do," he told his sister. "I'm not going to make it. But if you go back to school, and go to law school, and become my lawyer, I can do it."

Betty Anne couldn't believe what he was asking. She had dropped out of high school as a teenager. She had earned her GED—General Educational Development degree—by passing a written test. But to become a lawyer would require at least four years of college and three more years of law school.

"I don't care how long it takes if you promise me that you'll do it," Kenny insisted. "And I promise you that I will stay alive."

Really, there was no other choice, no Plan B, he said. "This is the only shot we got," he added. "We've got no money left. If you don't go, then I'm in here forever."

Betty Anne agreed, having no idea how she would make it work.

The rascals had made a pact.

Betty Anne Waters stands outside Aidan's Pub in Bristol, Rhode Island, in 2010. She worked there while she put herself through law school. Her employer, Aidan Graham, said of Waters, "She's always had this resilience, this passion."

9
School Days

By the time she made her promise to Kenny, Betty Anne Waters was 30 years old. She had two young sons and worked as a waitress. Going to law school seemed so unlikely she could barely imagine it. So she decided not to think too far ahead.

Instead she took one step at a time. First she enrolled in community college. She was the first in her family to do so. By 1989 she had earned an associate's degree in business.

But every time something went right, something else seemed to go wrong. The same year she got her associate's degree, her husband walked out on her. According to Waters, he resented her for returning to school.

Now a single mom, Betty Anne had to work even harder to keep her promise to Kenny. She transferred to Rhode Island College in Providence. To pay the bills she tended bar. She kept her schoolbooks nearby so she could read when business was slow.

By 1994 she had earned a bachelor's degree in economics and a master's degree in teaching. Still, she didn't take the next step for granted: law school. *What if I don't get in?* she wondered.

As it turned out, she didn't have to worry.

In 1995 Waters was admitted to Roger Williams University Law School in Bristol, Rhode Island. It was another leap forward, but with it came yet another setback. Her ex-husband took her to court and gained custody of their boys, Richard and Ben. It was his turn to be the primary parent, he claimed, and the court agreed.

Waters was devastated without the boys around. She felt isolated in law school among a sea of much younger students. The work seemed impossible. She dragged herself to her bar job, saw her sons occasionally, and fell asleep at night with mountains of law books spread around her on the bed. She began to doubt the path she had chosen.

I can't do this, she said to herself. *What am I thinking?*

Last Will And Testament 10-10-92

I Kenneth Waters being of sound mind leave all of my worldly possisions. Allso I will leave any money or property or both should any judgments that I win through any claims in any courtroom in Massachusetts or Rhode Island Allso I am a veteran of the united States army and Marine Corps. So I am entitiled to a military Burrilial at the expense of the United States of America. Goverment The Sole beneficiary to everything I have written in this will is My Sister Betty Ann Corentia or as known to me Betty Ann Waters. Allso Most important I am giving My Sister full athority on any dicisions concerning my Daughter Mandy Marsh. This allso includes any dicisions Weather its financial or personal concerning my Daughters Well Being.

Witness Kevin M. Liquorni
10-10-92

Kenneth William Waters
10/10 - 92

Kenny Waters was often depressed in jail. He wrote this will on October 10, 1992, and left his few belongings to his sister Betty Anne.

10
In the Genes

Betty Anne Waters tried to talk herself out of quitting law school. How could she desert Kenny? If she broke her promise, he could easily break his. His life seemed to rest in her hands.

She talked to Kenny twice a week, and he was relentless with his encouragement. "Betty Anne, I know you can do it," he told her repeatedly. "I know, I know, I know you can find something."

Her commitment to Kenny helped her get through the months without her two sons. Then, after a year with their father, Richard and Ben came back to live with her. Betty Anne welcomed them with an over-whelming feeling of relief.

Now in her second year of law school, she began to let herself believe there was hope for Kenny's case. She launched into a research project on a topic that just might hold the key to freeing her brother: DNA. That's the chain of molecules in the body that forms the genetic map for every living organism.

In the 13 years since Kenny had been convicted, police had started to use DNA to investigate crimes. Scientists could analyze tiny amounts of blood, skin, hair, saliva, or other bodily fluids. With the results, they could create a person's genetic profile. Like fingerprints, every person's profile is unique. And, like fingerprinting, DNA testing can be used to identify or eliminate suspects.

DNA evidence, Betty Anne realized, could prove Kenny's innocence. At the crime scene, police had identified two different types of blood—type B and type O. The victim's blood was type B. So the type O blood must have come from the killer. Kenny Waters had type O blood, but so did 48 percent of the population. Now, with new DNA testing, could Kenny be ruled out as Brow's murderer?

During her research, Betty Anne stumbled upon a legal group called the Innocence Project. Lawyers for the Innocence Project use DNA testing to free people who have been wrongly convicted of crimes. Betty Anne wrote a letter to them in November

I sent Kenny a copy of your letter explaining that DNA can provide strong evidence of one's innocence and that it could also provide proof of one's guilt. Kenny has absolutely no reservations about this testing and is waiting patiently to have DNA testing done to prove his innocence.

The day that my brother was unjustly convicted of this crime has changed not only his life, but mine. A high school dropout at the time, I went on to receive my Associates, Bachelors, and Masters degrees. Last May I received my Juris Doctorate degree and this month I will be sworn in as a member of the Rhode Island Bar Association. I have done everything in my power for the last seventeen years to prepare myself to prove my brother's innocence. By helping to insure the preservation of the crime scene evidence you will not only be helping to save my brother's life, but validating mine as well.

If I can assist your staff in my brother's case, please let me know. My family and I anxiously wait your response, as this has been the most important concern in our family for nearly seventeen years.

Sincerely,

Betty Anne Waters

Betty Anne Waters

In November 1998 Betty Anne Waters wrote this letter to the Innocence Project, asking for help. The Innocence Project was founded in 1992 by Barry Scheck and Peter J. Neufeld. Its mission is to use DNA testing to overturn wrongful convictions.

1998, explaining her brother's conviction and sentence.

"The crime took place in a very small town," she explained. Her troubled family was well known to the police. "I believe it was that familiarity that made my brother the ideal scapegoat for this horrific crime," she wrote.

Betty Anne's sincerity impressed the lawyers. But there was nothing they could do without evidence from the crime scene to compare to Kenny's DNA. They told Waters to get back to them if she found any evidence.

So much for that idea, Waters thought. It had been 15 years since the trial. By law the evidence could be destroyed after ten. "You just don't go in and ask, 'Can I have that old DNA?'" she later explained. "Because it just doesn't exist."

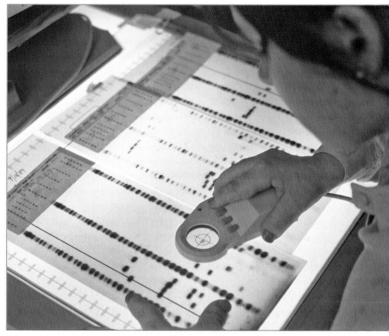

DNA charts are analyzed at a forensics laboratory. Since 1989, DNA tests have freed more than 250 wrongly convicted people. The average sentence served at the time they were freed was 13 years.

11

Unlocking the Case

Betty Anne Waters knew the odds were against her. But that was nothing new. For a decade she had been pursuing a degree she didn't think she could get. Now she was on a search for something that probably didn't exist. She started by badgering the courthouse clerks in Cambridge, where her brother had been convicted.

"That evidence has been destroyed," a clerk told her, because in all likelihood it had been. Betty Anne insisted that the clerk show her paperwork documenting the destruction. The clerk found none, so Waters kept pushing.

One day in 1998, a clerk agreed to rummage around in the musty basement archives. Betty Anne got a phone call: "Okay, yeah, we have something here," the clerk said. "There's a box down here with his name on it."

Waters rushed to the courthouse. She fumbled through the box. Inside were sealed plastic bags of evidence. They included the type O blood samples taken from the scene—the killer's blood. One bag contained a bloodstained piece of curtain from behind the kitchen sink. The killer had probably washed his or her hands and then dried them on the curtain.

Betty Anne rushed to call her brother.

This is the box of evidence from the Brow murder that Betty Anne Waters uncovered at the courthouse in Cambridge, Massachusetts, in 1998.

Prison had taken a terrible toll on Kenny Waters, now in his sixteenth year behind bars. He was balding and overweight and passed his days watching TV.

Kenny had been diagnosed with hepatitis C, a liver disease. To treat it, he needed to take a prison bus to a doctor. But Kenny was terrified of the inmates on the bus, so he remained untreated. He was sure he would die in prison.

Miserable beyond measure, Kenny could not imagine anything better than the news his sister gave him. "That's it!" he shouted. "The DNA!"

Betty Anne called the Innocence Project. She told Barry Scheck, one of the group's founders, about the new evidence. He was ready to help.

The process was painfully slow, but in 2000 a private lab did a DNA test on the evidence from the crime scene. They compared it to a blood sample from Kenny Waters. The samples did not match.

In March 2001 the Massachusetts State Police ran the test again—with the same results. The legal system, it appeared, had convicted the wrong man.

Betty Anne called her brother: "How would you like to come home tomorrow?"

The next day, on March 15, 2001, Kenny stood in the courthouse where he had been convicted of murder 18 years earlier. The judge set aside his murder conviction. Kenny could face trial again, but for now he walked out of the courthouse a free man.

"It's great to be free," he told a mob of reporters, with Betty Anne beaming at his side. Kenny longed for a hot bath, a soft mattress, ice cream, and a corned beef sandwich. "It's been 19 years and my whole family suffered unbelievably, and we're all just happy."

Kenny Waters was overwhelmed by new developments—cell phones, laptops, Starbucks, big box stores, and his own celebrity. Within 24 hours he went from his hard prison bed to the plush linens of a New York City hotel.

Back in Massachusetts, the case against Kenny fell apart. His two ex-girlfriends admitted they had lied. It came out that police officers had withheld fingerprints from the crime scene that didn't match Kenny's. Police also turned over Kenny's time cards from the diner, which would

Kenny and Betty Anne Waters speak at a press conference 11 days after Kenny's release from prison. "I think it's absolutely amazing that she's dedicated her life to this," Kenny said of his sister.

have given him an alibi for the time of the murder. When all of this information surfaced, prosecutors decided not to retry the case.

It was a perfect story for Hollywood, and movie producers started to call. Down-to-earth Betty Anne would have ignored them all, but Kenny insisted. The film *Conviction* was released in 2010, with Hilary Swank as Betty Anne. The movie ends on the thrilling day of Kenny's release.

The real-life ending was tragic for the Waters family. Six months after he was freed, Kenny fell 15 feet off a concrete wall. He died two weeks later from head injuries. Betty Anne was at his side. He was 47 years old and had spent a third of his life in jail.

To Betty Anne, it seemed about the cruelest thing that could happen. But she was able to see a silver lining. At least Kenny had died free and happy, she said, after the best six months of his life.

After the movie opened, Betty Anne took a leave from her job at the bar. She traveled the country, talking about the case. "I definitely lost faith in the system," she acknowledged.

Kenny's estate and the Innocence Project won $10.7 million in damages from the town of Ayer for false imprisonment. The judge wrote that Kenny had lived in extreme misery for 18 years, deprived of every pleasure an ordinary life could offer.

The day after his release, someone asked Kenny Waters just how much he loved his sister. "Oh, with all my heart and soul," he said. "She's—she's—she's it. Without her, there'd be no life left."

Betty Anne Waters sheds a tear at the opening of
Conviction, the movie about her struggle to prove
her brother's innocence. Waters said of the film,
"It will put a face to the issue . . . It will help
people understand how an innocent person winds
up in prison."

Betty Anne Waters

Born:

August 1954

Grew up:

Ayer, Massachusetts, as one of nine children

Graduate of:

Rogers Williams University School of Law, 1998

Life's work:

Became a lawyer to free her innocent brother from
prison

Her voice on the record:

Wrote letter to the Innocence Project, convincing the
organization to help with her brother's appeal; worked
with writers of the film *Conviction* to make her story
into a script

Day job:

General manager and part-owner of Aidan's Pub in
Bristol, Rhode Island

Volunteers for:

The Innocence Project, the organization that helped
with her brother's release

She says:

"[After hearing my story,] hopefully people will look at
the justice system and make it a little better. We don't
have a bad system, but we can make it so much better.
I live for the day that I get a call that . . . because of this
movie another innocent person went free. That would
make my world."

A Conversation with Author
C. J. Midland

Q *What was your process for researching this book?*

A I read many books and periodicals about Medgar and Myrlie Evers, including three books written by Myrlie Evers-Williams. For my research on Betty Anne Waters, I read lots of newspaper and magazine stories. Also, the Innocence Project has posted photos and original documents related to Kenny Waters's case on its website. And I interviewed Betty Anne Waters.

Q *How did you go about writing this book?*

A Outlines help me think through the shape of a story—beginning, middle, and end. They give me a map and a security blanket. Even if I don't really know what's next, I can look at the map and keep going. After that, it's about finding the life-changing moments or moments of high emotion or drama.

Q *Is it difficult to write about someone without being able to interview them?*

A I like being able to talk with the subject; it gives me more of a feeling for their life. I was not able to speak with Myrlie Evers-Williams, but she's written so extensively about her life and granted so many interviews that I'm not sure I could have gotten more emotion or detail than what she has already revealed.

Q *What aspects of the two stories touched you most?*

A When Medgar Evers taught his children self-defense—that was just chilling. And the fact that the children witnessed their father's death was very upsetting. I was also moved by Kenneth Waters's absolute faith in his sister.

Q *Why did the justice system get it so wrong? What parallels do you see between the two cases?*

A In both cases, I think you see how the justice system reflects a time and a place, some aspect of the culture as a whole. Everyone in the Evers case, from the police to the witnesses to the jury, mirrored the vicious racism of Mississippi in 1963.

The case of Kenneth Waters probably also involved bias. He was poor and uneducated, with a criminal past. In Betty Anne's view, the unspoken assumption was that he seemed like the kind of guy who could have killed—therefore he must have been the killer.

Q *What do Betty Anne Waters and Myrlie Evers-Williams have in common? How are they different?*

A Both were young single moms dealing with the intricacies of a murder case. Both found an inner strength and conviction that drove them for decades. Both were also driven by their devotion to loved ones—a husband and a brother. Both came into their own during their quests.

But their stories unfold in different moments in history, in different parts of the country, with different obstacles. Myrlie Evers-Williams came from an educated, southern, black, middle-class family, and she was fighting racism. Betty Anne Waters came from a white family in the northeast that was relatively poor and uneducated, and she struggled to rise above class limitations.

Q *Do you think these stories are about more than the personal stories of two remarkable women?*

A Myrlie Evers-Williams's life and her quest for justice after Medgar's death have an epic feel or scope. The themes are about the deeply segregated South, the backlash against the Civil Rights Movement in Mississippi, and later the atonement for this racist past.

Betty Anne Waters's story *is* about one woman's amazing quest, but it also reveals the fallibility of the

criminal justice system. And I don't mean to suggest
that this is a small theme. Capital punishment
has been under more scrutiny because of these
exonerations, and some states have abolished the
death penalty. That's huge.

Q *Was your opinion of the justice system in the U.S.
affected by your research for this book?*

A I have written about the justice system
before—about how a police department in Oakland,
California, ignored the rape cases of poor, nonwhite
women with criminal pasts. And I wrote about the
severe punishment meted out to a group of battered
women who killed their abusers. These were stories
about patterns of bias and about where the criminal
justice system broke down.

Q *How might the lives and work of Evers-Williams
and Waters engage others?*

A I think it takes people like Betty Anne Waters
and Myrlie Evers-Williams to stand up for what's
right. And I think people do respond to these quests.
As Evers-Williams has said, people yearn to see
justice carried out in such cases. I absolutely agree.

What to Read Next

Fiction

House Rules, Jodi Picoult. (544 pages) *Jacob Hunt, a teenager with Asperger's Syndrome, is always showing up at crime scenes and giving advice to the police. Then the police accuse him of murder.*

To Kill a Mockingbird, Harper Lee. (284 pages) *A lawyer struggles against prejudice, violence, and hypocrisy in a southern town in the 1930s.*

Monster, Walter Dean Myers. (281 pages) *A teenager is on trial for being involved in the shooting of a convenience-store owner, but he may just have been an innocent bystander.*

The Rock and the River, Kekla Magoon. (304 pages) *Sam Childs, a teenager in Chicago in 1968, has to decide whether to support the Black Panthers or continue demonstrating peacefully within the Civil Rights Movement.*

Nonfiction

Freedom's Children: Young Civil Rights Activists Tell Their Own Stories, edited by Ellen S. Levine. (192 pages) *This book presents 30 first-person accounts written by people who were young activists in the Civil Rights Movement.*

Freedom Riders: John Lewis and Jim Zwerg on the Front Lines of the Civil Rights Movement, Ann Bausum. (80 pages) *A black southerner and a white northerner fight together for a common cause in the Civil Rights Movement.*

Guilty By a Hair! Real-life DNA Matches!, Anna Prokos. (64 pages) *This book explains the scientific background of DNA evidence and how it has been used to solve real crimes.*

Surviving Justice: America's Wrongly Convicted and Exonerated, compiled by Lola Vollen and Dave Eggers. (512 pages) *This book tells the moving stories of 13 people who went to prison for crimes they didn't commit.*

Books

Mississippi Challenge, Mildred Pitts Walter. (256 pages) *Walter documents the struggles of black people in Mississippi from before the Civil War through the 1960s.*

Not Guilty, George Sullivan. (148 pages) *This book presents many examples of innocent people who have been convicted of crimes in the United States.*

Films and Videos

Eyes on the Prize: America's Civil Rights Years 1954-1965 (1987) *This PBS documentary series is considered the definitive film about the Civil Rights Movement in the United States.*

Ghosts of Mississippi (1996) *This movie tells the story of the trial of Medgar Evers's killer. It was nominated for two Oscars.*

Websites

www.innocenceproject.org
This is the website of the Innocence Project, an organization dedicated to clearing the names of people who have been wrongfully convicted.

www.eyeneer.tv/video/rock/only-a-pawn-in-their-game
This is a 1963 performance of Bob Dylan singing the song he wrote about the murder of Medgar Evers.

www.splcenter.org
The Southern Poverty Law Center is an important civil rights organization. This site presents the history and purpose of the movement and offers opportunities to get involved.

Glossary

alibi (AL-i-bye) *noun* a claim that a person accused of a crime was somewhere else when the crime was committed

assassin (uh-SASS-uhn) *noun* someone who kills a well-known or powerful person

backwater (BAK-waw-tur) *adjective* regarded as isolated or backward

boycott (BOI-kot) *noun* a refusal to do business with a person or organization as an act of protest

Citizens' Councils (SIT-i-zuhnz KOUN-suhlz) *noun* an organization of white supremacists, founded in 1954, that opposed racial integration

diction (DIK-shuhn) *noun* the choice and use of words and phrases in speech or writing

DNA (DEE EN AY) *noun* short for "deoxyribonucleic acid," the chain of molecules that carries the genetic code that gives living things their characteristics

dysfunctional (diss-FUHNGK-shuh-nul) *adjective* having abnormal or unhealthy behavior within a group or family

exoneration (eks-OHN-ur-AY-shuhn) *noun* recognition that a person accused of a crime is innocent

forensic (fuh-REHN-zik) *adjective* describing the science used to investigate and solve crimes

Jim Crow (JIM KROH) *noun* the term for the segregation laws and customs that oppressed blacks after the Civil War through the 1960s

mistrial (MISS-trye-uhl) *noun* a trial that becomes invalid due to errors in procedure or the inability of the jurors to agree on a verdict

molecule (MOL-uh-kyool) *noun* the smallest part of a substance that contains all the chemical properties of that substance; molecules are groups of atoms

NAACP (EN DUH-buhl AY SEE PEE) *noun* short for "National Association for the Advancement of Colored People," an organization founded to protect and expand the civil rights of African Americans

potential (puh-TEN-shihl) *noun* the possibility of becoming or happening

scapegoat (SKAPE-goht) *noun* someone who is unfairly made to take all the blame for something

segregation (seg-ruh-GAY-shuhn) *noun* the act or practice of keeping people or groups apart

sit-in (SIT-in) *noun* the act of sitting in the seats or on the floor of an establishment as a means of organized protest

solitary (SOL-uh-ter-ee) *noun* the locking up of a prisoner away from other prisoners as a form of punishment or for the prisoner's protection

unanimous (yoo-NAN-uh-muhss) *adjective* agreed on by everyone involved

Sources

LONG ROAD TO JUSTICE

Watch Me Fly: What I Learned on the Way to Becoming the Woman I Was Mean to Be, Myrlie Evers-Williams with Melinda Blau. Boston: Little, Brown, 1999. (includin quotes on pages 14, 22, 23, 36, 47, 52, 54, 58, 59)

"30 Years Later, 3rd Trial Begins in Evers Killing," Ronald Smothers. *New York Times,* January 28, 1994. (including quote on page 55)

The Autobiography of Medgar Evers: A Hero's Life and Legacy Revealed Throug His Writings, Letters, and Speeches, Myrlie Evers-Williams and Manning Marable. New York: Basic Civitas Books, 2006. (including quotes on pages 36, 37, 40)

"Beckwith Case a Mistrial; Jury Was 7-5 for Acquittal," John Herbers. *New York Times,* February 8, 1964. (including quote on page 43)

"Caldera's Stories of Change with Myrlie Evers-Williams." YouTube.com, September 29, 2010. (including quote on page 55)

"Creating Jim Crow," Ronald L. F. Davis. www.JimCrowHistory.org.

For Us, the Living, Myrlie Evers with William Peters. Jackson, MS: Banner Books, 1996. (including quotes on pages 15, 35, 40, 41, 58)

Ghosts of Mississippi, Maryanne Vollers. Boston: Little, Brown, 1995. (including quo on pages 23, 40, 42, 49)

"Jury Convicts Beckwith in '63 Slaying of Evers," Curtis Wilkie. *Boston Globe,* February 6, 199 (including quote on page 54)

"The Legacy of Medgar Evers: 40 Years after Civil Rights Leader's Death, a Changed Mississippi." NPR's *All Things Considered,* June 10, 2003.

Never Too Late: A Prosecutor's Story of Justice in the Medgar Evers Case, Bobby DeLaughter. New York: Scribner, 2001.

Of Long Memory: Mississippi and the Murder of Medgar Evers, Adam Nossiter. Reading, MA: Addison-Wesley, 1994.

"Reliving the Evers Death: Mississippi Haunted by '63 Murder of Black," Laura Parker Washington. *Washington Post,* February 9, 1991.

"Trials and Transformation: Myrlie Evers' 30-Year Fight to Convict Medgar's Accused Killer," Karen Grigsby Gates. *Emerge,* February 1994. (including quote on page 36)

"The Widow Gets Her Verdict," Claudia Dreifus. *New York Times Magazine,* Novembe 27, 1994. (including quotes on pages 4, 41, 49, 56)

THE PACT

Author's interview with Betty Anne Waters in 2010. (including quotes on pages 5, 63, 6 68, 71, 76, 91, 92, 99)

"Academy Award-Winner Hilary Swank Takes on Story of Wrongful Conviction," Michelle Martin. NPR's *Tell Me More,* October 14, 2010. (including quotes on pages 78, 79)

"After 18 Years in Prison 'It's Great to Be Free,'" Farah Stockman. *Boston Globe*, March 16, 2001. (including quote on page 97)

"Ayer Murderer Gets Life Term," Thomas Grillo. *Lowell Sun*, May 12, 1983.

"Ayer Settles Over Wrongful '83 Slay Conviction," Lisa Redmond. *Lowell Sun*, July 15, 2009.

"Betty Anne Waters," Bryant Gumbel. *The Early Show*, March 16, 2001. (including quote on page 79)

"Betty Anne Waters: Hilary Swank's *Conviction* Real-Life Inspiration," Joel D. Amos. *She Knows Entertainment*, October 19, 2010. (including quote on page 101)

"Betty Anne Waters, Sister of Convicted Murderer Kenneth Waters, Becomes Lawyer to Free Her Brother," Diane Sawyer. *Good Morning America*, March 16, 2001. (including quotes on pages 89, 94, 99)

"Blood Connections: Driven to Become a Lawyer, R.I. Woman Finds Evidence to Free Her Brother," Farah Stockman. *Boston Globe*, March 15, 2001.

"Brother's Keeper," Chris Wallace with Sylvia Chase. *ABC Primetime News*, March 22, 2011. (including quotes on pages 77, 83, 85)

"Conviction is R.I. Story of Salvation," Michael Janusonis. *Providence Journal*, October 10, 2010. (including quote on page 68)

"Court to Consider Deterioration of Man Wrongfully Convicted in Ayer Killing," Lisa Redmond. *Lowell Sun*, July 19, 2009.

"From Waitress to Brother's Savior, then Hollywood Hero," Robin Pogrebin. *New York Times*, October 13, 2010.

The Innocence Project. www.InnocenceProject.org. (including quote on page 89)

"Jury Deliberating Fate of Ayer Man," Thomas Grillo. *Lowell Sun*, May 11, 1983.

"'Muddy Waters' Runs Free: Convict Out After 19 Years," Dave Wedge. *Boston Herald*, March 16, 2001.

"New Evidence and a New Life: Sister's Crusade Overturns Brother's Murder Conviction," Greta Van Sustern and Bill Delaney. *The Point with Greta Van Sustern*, March 15, 2001. (including quote on page 96)

"Reluctant Hero," John Larrabee and Russ Olivo. *Rhode Island Monthly*, February 2010. (including quotes on pages 80, 100).

"Sister Act: How a Committed Sister Freed Her Brother From Prison," Sarah Buscher. *Irish America*, September 30, 2001. (including quote on page 82)

"Two Testify Waters Admitting to Killing," Thomas Grillo. *Sunday Sun*, May 8, 1983. (including quote on page 74)

"Waters Once Served Time, Judge Told," Patricia Montminy. *Lowell Sun*. (including quote on page 70)

"Woman's 18-Year Quest Edges Brother to Freedom," Jerry O'Brien. *Providence Journal-Bulletin*, March 15, 2001. (including quote on page 95)

Index